From Your Friends At The MAILBOX®

Persuasive Writing

Grades 4–6

Project Manager:
Elizabeth H. Lindsay

Writer:
Stephanie Willett-Smith

Contributing Editors:
Scott Lyons, Cindy Mondello, Jennifer Munnerlyn

Art Coordinator:
Clevell Harris

Artists:
Pam Crane, Teresa R. Davidson, Clevell Harris, Rob Mayworth,
Rebecca Saunders, Barry Slate, Donna K. Teal

Cover Artists:
Nick Greenwood and Kimberly Richard

www.themailbox.com

Writing Works!™

©2000 by THE EDUCATION CENTER, INC.
All rights reserved.
ISBN #1-56234-342-4

Manufactured in the United States

10 9 8 7 6 5 4 3

Table of Contents

About This Book

What Is Persuasive Writing?

In *persuasive writing,* a writer tries to convince, or *persuade,* a reader that his or her opinion is the best one. The writer states an opinion at the beginning of the writing; gives details or reasons that prove, explain, or support this opinion in the body of the writing; and concludes the writing by restating the opinion. When writing a persuasive paragraph, it is important to state facts to support an opinion.

Develop and enhance your students' persuasive-writing skills with this easy-to-use collection of 20 two-page lessons. *Writing Works!—Persuasive* contains everything you need to supplement a successful writing program in your classroom.

Each two-page lesson contains the following:

- A motivating writing prompt
- Simple steps for teaching the prewriting and writing stages of each lesson
- A student reproducible that is either a graphic organizer used in the prewriting stages or a pattern on which students write their final drafts
- Suggestions for publishing or displaying students' work

Also included:

- A reproducible proofreading checklist for the student
- A reproducible persuasive-writing assessment for the teacher
- 16 extra persuasive-writing prompts
- A student reproducible containing 13 commonly used editing symbols

Other books in the Writing Works! series:
- *Writing Works!—Narrative*
- *Writing Works!—Clarification*
- *Writing Works!—Descriptive*
- *Writing Works!—Explanatory*
- *Writing Works!—Expressive*

To School or Not to School?

Imagine you heard a news report in which a government official announced the possibility of year-round schooling in the United States. Write a letter to the official persuading him to make or not make year-round schooling a requirement.

Think It!

1. Read the following statements to students:
   - You should not smoke because it's bad.
   - You should not smoke because the surgeon general has found that smoking may cause cancer.

   If your students were trying to convince someone to quit smoking, ask them which statement they would choose and why.

2. Point out that when attempting to convince someone of something, it is important to state facts to support your opinion. Call on a student volunteer to describe a time when he attempted to convince someone to agree with his opinion. Have the student explain the facts used to help persuade the individual.

3. Explain to students that when writing to persuade, the writer tries to convince the reader(s) that his opinion is the best one. He states his opinion at the beginning; gives details or reasons that prove, explain, or support it; and concludes by restating his opinion.

4. Read aloud the prompt above, display it on a transparency, or write it on the board.

5. Give each student a copy of page 5. Instruct the student to use the reproducible to organize his thoughts and ideas about year-round schooling.

Write It!

1. Instruct the student to use the information recorded on page 5 to help write his persuasive letter on another sheet of paper. Remind the student to include a topic sentence, at least three strong supporting details, and a concluding sentence.

2. Direct the student to proofread and edit his work carefully. Encourage students to swap papers to peer-edit. After all corrections have been made, direct the student to write his final version on another sheet of paper.

3. If desired, give each student a 9" x 12" sheet of construction paper and a craft stick. Direct the student to create a poster showing his opinion about year-round schooling. Then have him glue the poster to the craft stick. Display students' posters and final versions on a wall or bulletin board titled "To School or Not to School?"

Name _____

Persuasive writing

To School or Not to School?

Opinion/Topic Sentence:
_____
_____

Supporting Details:

1. _____
_____

2. _____
_____

3. _____
_____

4. _____
_____

5. _____
_____

Conclusion: _____
_____

©2000 The Education Center, Inc. • *Writing Works!* • Persuasive • TEC2310

5

Destination: Best Vacation

PROMPT

Your favorite vacation spot is the tops! Imagine that you're there, and then write a postcard persuading a friend that it's the best place in the world to vacation.

Think It!

1. Have each student imagine her favorite vacation spot and think about the reasons that make it her favorite. Call on student volunteers to share what makes their favorite vacation spots so remarkable (such as having the best restaurants, exciting activities, and magnificent scenery). List their responses on the board.

2. Tell students your favorite vacation spot. Give reasons why it is your favorite, including some facts and some opinions. Point out to students that if you were attempting to convince someone that this is the best spot, it would be important to state facts to support your opinion.

3. Explain to students that when writing to persuade someone, the writer tries to convince the reader(s) that her opinion is the best one. She states her opinion at the beginning; gives details or reasons that prove, explain, or support it; and concludes by restating her opinion.

4. Read aloud the prompt above, display it on a transparency, or write it on the board.

5. Give each student a copy of page 7. In the space provided on the postcard, have each student draw a picture of the spot she's imagined, including five labeled details that show why her spot is a great one.

Write It!

1. Instruct the student to use her picture on page 7 to help write a postcard persuading a friend that her vacation spot is the best one. Have the student write her postcard on a separate sheet of paper. Remind the student to include a topic sentence, three strong supporting details, and a concluding sentence.

2. Direct the student to proofread and edit her work carefully. Encourage students to swap papers to peer-edit. After all corrections have been made, have the student write her final copy in the space provided on page 7. Then instruct each student to cut out the pattern along the bold lines, fold it, and then glue it to make a postcard.

3. If desired, use a shoebox and construction paper to create a class mailbox. Place students' postcards in the box, and then set it up at a center so that students can read the postcards during free time.

Name ____

Destination: Best Vacation

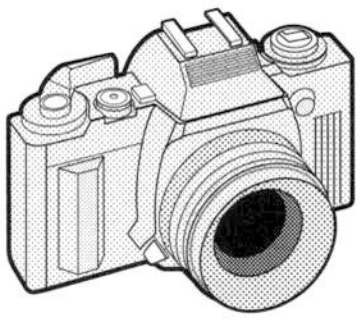

Top Vacation Destination

Tom Travel
123 Vacation Street
Leisureville, LA 65432

Fold here.

____

____

____

____

____

____

____

____

____

____

____

VISIT

____
(Name of vacation spot)

Cast Your Votes!

PROMPT *Your school is getting ready to hold its annual student council elections, and you've decided to run for office. Write a speech persuading your classmates to vote for you as class president.*

VOTE
TOMMY
FOR
CLASS
PRESIDENT

Think It!

1. Challenge students to recall the names of past or present U.S. presidential candidates. Have them name the good leadership qualities that these candidates possessed. Record their responses on the board.

2. Explain to students that part of running a successful campaign is having a candidate who is able to convince the voters that he or she is the best person for the job. Ask students to determine which of the following is more convincing:
   - When I was leader of my state, it became a better place in which to live.
   - When I was leader of my state, I cut taxes and provided computers for every classroom.
   Point out to students that if they were attempting to convince someone that they would be good leaders, it would be important to state facts to support their opinions.

3. Explain to students that when writing to persuade, the writer tries to convince the reader(s) that his opinion is the best one. He states his opinion at the beginning; gives details or reasons that prove, explain, or support it; and concludes by restating his opinion.

4. Read aloud the prompt above, display it on a transparency, or write it on the board.

5. Give each student a copy of page 9. Instruct the student to use the reproducible to organize his thoughts and ideas for his speech. Encourage him to remember what his classmates thought were the qualities of good leaders—they're the voters!

Write It!

1. Have the student use the information recorded on page 9 to help write his speech. Remind the student to include a topic sentence, at least three strong supporting details, and a concluding sentence.

2. Direct the student to proofread and edit his work carefully. Encourage students to swap papers to peer-edit. After all corrections have been made, have the student write his final copy on another sheet of paper.

3. If desired, have each student read his speech to the rest of the class. Then have the class vote for the most persuasive speech by casting ballots in a mock election. Hail to the chief!

Name_____ *Persuasive writing*

Cast Your Votes!

Opinion/Topic Sentence: _____

_____

Reason 1:

_____

_____

_____

Reason 2:

_____

_____

Reason 3:

_____

_____

_____

VOTE!

Reason 4:

_____

_____

_____

Reason 5:

_____

_____

Conclusion: _____

_____

An Invention Convention

PROMPT At the annual Invention Convention, you are asked to head up a committee to select the most important invention of all time. Write a paragraph persuading the committee that the invention you picked is the most important.

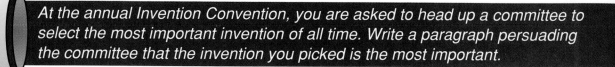

Think It!

1. With your students' help, list a few of the greatest inventions of all time on the board (for example, the automobile, lightbulb, and computer). Circle the word *automobile*. Call on several students to share their thoughts about why this invention is important.

2. Write the following sentences about the automobile on the board:
   - The automobile is the most important invention because it makes life easier.
   - The automobile is the most important invention because it can carry people and heavy loads faster than earlier forms of transportation.

   Point out to students that if you were attempting to convince someone that the automobile was the most important invention of all time, it would be important to state facts to support your opinion.

3. Explain to students that when writing to persuade someone, the writer tries to convince the reader(s) that her opinion is the best one. She states her opinion at the beginning; gives details or reasons that prove, explain, or support it; and concludes by restating her opinion.

4. Read aloud the prompt above, display it on a transparency, or write it on the board.

5. Tell each student to select an invention other than the automobile that she thinks is the most important. Give each student a copy of page 11. In the space provided, have the student draw this invention and then use the rest of the reproducible to organize her thoughts and ideas about why it is important.

Write It!

1. Instruct each student to use the information recorded on page 11 to help write her persuasive paragraph on another sheet of paper. Remind the student to include a topic sentence, at least three strong supporting details, and a concluding sentence.

2. Direct the student to proofread and edit her work carefully. Encourage students to swap papers to peer-edit. After all corrections have been made, instruct the student to write her final version on another sheet of paper.

3. If desired, make a large grid using a sheet of chart paper. Post the grid in the center of a bulletin board and display students' final versions around it. As a class, use the grid to make a bar graph showing which inventions were chosen. Then have students (the committee!) use the graph to find out which invention the majority of them thought was the most important.

Invention Convention

The Most Important Invention of All Time

Topic Sentence:

The most important invention of all time is the

_____ .

Reason 1: _____

_____

_____

Reason 2: _____

_____

_____

Reason 3: _____

_____

_____

Reason 4: _____

_____

_____

Reason 5: _____

_____

Most important invention? Hmmm...

Conclusion: _____

_____

May the Best Book Win!

 **PROMPT**

Have you read any good books this year? The Better Books Club is about to present its annual Readers' Choice Award. Write a letter to the club persuading its members that the book you've chosen deserves to be given this honor.

Think It!

1. Have students name the best books they have recently read. Record their responses on the board. Then have the students give reasons why they like the books.

2. Tell students what your favorite children's book is. Give reasons why it is your favorite, including some facts and opinions. Point out to students that if you were attempting to convince someone that this was the best book, it would be important to state facts to support your opinion.

3. Explain to students that when writing to persuade someone, the writer tries to convince the reader(s) that his opinion is the best one. He states his opinion at the beginning; gives details or reasons that prove, explain, or support it; and concludes by restating his opinion.

4. Read aloud the prompt above, display it on a transparency, or write it on the board. Then give each student a copy of page 13.

5. Direct each student to use the reproducible to organize his thoughts and ideas about his chosen book.

Write It!

1. Tell each student to use the information recorded on page 13 to help write a letter (on another sheet of paper) persuading the club that his book should be given the award. Remind the student to include a topic sentence, at least three strong supporting details, and a concluding sentence.

2. Direct the student to proofread and edit his work carefully. Encourage students to swap papers to peer-edit. After all the corrections have been made, have him write his final draft on another sheet of paper.

3. If desired, give each student a 9" x 12" sheet of white construction paper. Direct the student to fold the sheet in half to create a book jacket. On the front side, have each student title his jacket and illustrate it with a scene or character from his favorite book. Then have him write his finished letter on the inside. Display the finished projects on a covered table with the jackets standing open.

May the Best Book Win!

Book Title: _____

Opinion/Topic Sentence: _____

_____

Supporting Details:

1.

2.

3.

4.

5.

Conclusion: _____

_____

Development Dilemma

Your city's planners are trying to decide whether or not to build a shopping mall on a local area of land. Although the mall is going to provide much-needed shopping, the area is home to several species of animals. Write a letter to the planners persuading them to build or not to build.

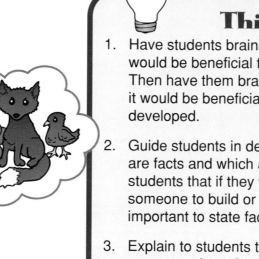

Think It!

1. Have students brainstorm a list of reasons why it would be beneficial to build a new shopping mall. Then have them brainstorm a list of reasons why it would be beneficial to keep a piece of land undeveloped.

2. Guide students in deciding which of their reasons are facts and which are opinions. Point out to students that if they were attempting to convince someone to build or not to build, it would be important to state facts to support their opinions.

3. Explain to students that when writing to persuade someone, the writer tries to convince the reader(s) that her opinion is the best one. She states her opinion at the beginning; gives details or reasons that prove, explain, or support it; and concludes by restating her opinion.

4. Read aloud the prompt above, display it on a transparency, or write it on the board.

5. Give each student a copy of page 15. Direct the student to use the reproducible to organize her thoughts and ideas about the land development.

Write It!

1. Have the student use the information recorded on page 15 to help write a letter persuading the planners to support her position. Remind the student to include a topic sentence, at least three strong supporting details, and a concluding sentence.

2. Direct the student to proofread and edit her work carefully. Encourage students to swap papers to peer-edit. After all corrections have been made, have the student write her final copy of the letter on a separate sheet of paper.

3. If desired, invite each student to share her completed letter. Then divide students into groups based on their opinions. Allow the two opposing groups to hold a debate. Have the class vote on which group more clearly argues its point.

Development Dilemma

To build...

...or not to build?

Opinion/Topic Sentence: _____
_____

Reason 1
_____
_____
_____
_____

Reason 4
_____
_____
_____
_____

Reason 2
_____
_____
_____
_____

Reason 3
_____
_____
_____
_____

Conclusion: _____
_____

We're in the Money!

Think It!

1. Ask each student to think of an item—such as a big-screen TV, a stereo system, or a basketball goal—that he would like his family to purchase for their home. Then call on a student volunteer to share his item and reasons why his family should purchase it. For example, a new basketball goal might be the focus of family time and could provide outdoor exercise.

2. Share with students one item that you would like to purchase for your home. Give reasons for your choice, including some facts and some opinions. Point out to students that when attempting to convince someone of something, it is important to state facts to support your opinion.

3. Explain to students that when writing to persuade someone, the writer tries to convince the reader(s) that his opinion is the best one. He states his opinion at the beginning; gives details or reasons that prove, explain, or support it; and concludes by restating his opinion.

4. Read aloud the prompt above, display it on a transparency, or write it on the board.

5. Give each student a copy of page 17. Direct the student to use the reproducible to organize his thoughts and ideas about how his family should spend the money.

Write It!

1. Instruct the student to use the information recorded on page 17 to help write his persuasive letter. Remind the student to include a topic sentence, at least three strong supporting details, and a concluding sentence.

2. Direct the student to proofread and edit his work carefully. Encourage students to swap papers to peer-edit. After all corrections have been made, have the student write his final copy of the letter on a large index card.

3. If desired, punch a hole in each card and then bind the cards with a metal ring. Store the cards in a paper or canvas "money bag" for students to read during free time.

Name _____ *Persuasive writing*

We're in the Money!

Opinion/Topic Sentence:

_____

_____

Reason 1:

_____
_____
_____
_____
_____
_____

Reason 2:

_____
_____
_____
_____
_____
_____

Reason 3:

_____
_____
_____
_____
_____
_____
_____

Reason 4:

_____
_____
_____
_____
_____

Reason 5:

_____
_____
_____
_____

$ **Conclusion:** _____ $

_____

$ _____ $

Let's Eat!

PROMPT *You've been hired by your favorite fast-food restaurant to help write an advertisement promoting it. Write a paragraph persuading people that this restaurant is the best place to eat.*

Think It!

1. As a class, brainstorm a list of fast-food restaurants. Have volunteers name reasons why each restaurant is appealing, and list their responses on the board. Then have students identify which reasons are based on fact and which are based on opinion. Point out to students that when attempting to convince someone of something, it is important to state facts to support your opinion.

2. Explain to students that when writing to persuade, the writer tries to convince the reader(s) that her opinion is the best one. She states her opinion at the beginning; gives details or reasons that prove, explain, or support it; and concludes by restating her opinion.

3. Read aloud the prompt above, display it on a transparency, or write it on the board.

4. Give each student one copy of page 19. Have the student choose her favorite fast-food restaurant from the list on the board and then use the reproducible to organize her thoughts and ideas.

Write It!

1. Instruct each student to use the information recorded on page 19 to help write a paragraph persuading people that her chosen restaurant is the best place to eat. Remind the student to include a topic sentence, at least three strong supporting details, and a concluding sentence. For added fun, encourage each student to use catchy words and phrases in her paragraph (for example: *mouthwatering, delicious, fast, friendly, no hassle, clean,* etc.).

2. Direct the student to proofread and edit her work carefully. Encourage students to swap papers to peer-edit. After all corrections have been made, have each student write her final copy on another sheet of paper or a large index card.

3. If desired, provide each student with a quiet space where she can read aloud her paragraph into a tape recorder, as if she were a radio announcer. Play each recording for the class; then poll students to see which "ad" is the most persuasive!

Let's Eat!

My Favorite Restaurant: _____

Topic Sentence: _____

Supporting Details:

1

2

3

4

Conclusion:

FRIES

Dressing Dilemma

PROMPT *School uniforms—yea or nay? Your principal has asked you to give a speech to the school board about wearing required school uniforms. Write a paragraph persuading the school board to vote for or against this issue.*

Think It!

1. Present to your students a school-related issue, such as "School breakfast should be served," or "Students should not change classes for different subjects." Then poll students, asking them to vote yea or nay on the issue.

2. Have student volunteers share their reasons for voting yes or no, listing their responses on the board. Then have students identify the reasons that are factual. Point out to students that when attempting to convince someone of something, it is important to state facts to support your opinion.

3. Explain to students that when writing to persuade, the writer tries to convince the reader(s) that his opinion is the best one. He states his opinion at the beginning; gives details or reasons that prove, explain, or support it; and concludes by restating his opinion.

4. Read aloud the prompt above, display it on a transparency, or write it on the board.

5. Give each student a copy of page 21. Have him use the reproducible to organize his thoughts and ideas about why students should or should not wear school uniforms.

Write It!

1. Instruct each student to use the information recorded on page 21 to help write his paragraph. Remind the student to include a topic sentence, at least three strong supporting details, and a concluding sentence.

2. Direct the student to proofread and edit his work carefully. Encourage students to swap papers to peer-edit. After all corrections have been made, have each student write his final copy on another sheet of paper.

3. If desired, give each student a sheet of 9" x 12" construction paper and a coat hanger. Direct the student to glue his paragraph to the sheet of construction paper and then tape the paper to the bottom of the hanger. Attach two lengths of string or yarn to a wall, labeling one string "Yea" and the other "Nay." Post students' hangers on the appropriate string.

Dressing Dilemma

BALLOT

Please check one.

I vote [ ] for

[ ] against

mandatory school uniforms.

Topic Sentence: _____

_____

Supporting   Details:

1

2

3

4

5

Conclusion: _____

_____

Are You Ready to Rock?

PROMPT *Your friend has asked you to join a band and it's music to your ears! Write a letter persuading your parents to let you join the band.*

Think It!

1. As a class, brainstorm different kinds of music and favorite bands. Ask students to tell the benefits of being in a band. (For example, it might be fun and they would learn to play an instrument.) List students' responses on the board. Point out to students that if they were attempting to convince someone to let them join a band, it would be important to state facts to support their opinions.

2. Explain to students that when writing to persuade, the writer tries to convince the reader(s) that her opinion is the best one. She states her opinion at the beginning; gives details or reasons that prove, explain, or support it; and concludes by restating her opinion.

3. Read aloud the prompt above, display it on a transparency, or write it on the board.

4. Give each student a copy of page 23. Have her use the top portion of the reproducible to organize her thoughts and ideas.

Write It!

1. Instruct each student to use the information recorded on page 23 to help write a letter persuading her parents to let her join a band. Remind the student to include a topic sentence, at least three strong supporting details, and a concluding sentence.

2. Direct the student to proofread and edit her work carefully. Encourage students to swap papers to peer-edit. After all corrections have been made, have each student write her final copy in the space provided on the bottom portion of page 23.

3. If desired, give each student a 9" x 12" sheet of light-colored construction paper. Direct the student to draw and cut out her favorite musical instrument. Post students' instruments along with their final copies around the room so students can applaud each others' persuasive efforts.

Name ______________________________ *Persuasive writing*

Are You Ready to Rock?

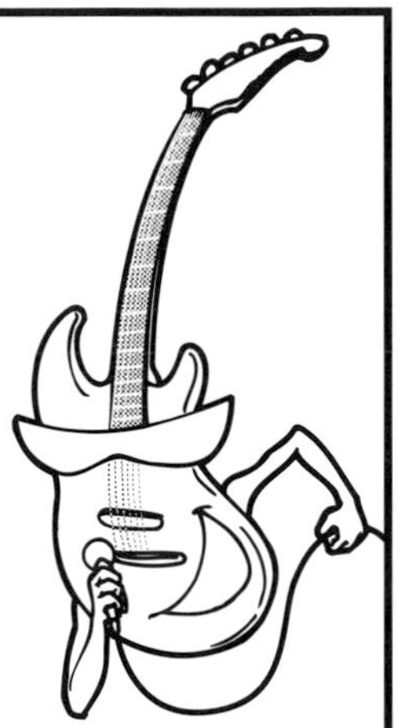

Opinion/Topic Sentence: ______________________________

____

Supporting Details:

1. ______________________________

   ____

2. ______________________________

   ____

3. ______________________________

   ____

4. ______________________________

   ____

Conclusion: ______________________________

____

____

____

____

____

____

____

____

____

____

Angling for an Allowance

 **PROMPT** *Who wouldn't want a little extra spending money? Write a paragraph persuading your parents to give you an allowance each week.*

Think It!

1. Ask students to raise their hands if they receive an allowance. Invite students to share the jobs they perform or responsibilities they have to earn this money.

2. Brainstorm with students the benefits of receiving an allowance (for example, having extra spending money and learning to save money). List student responses on the board. Point out to students that if they were attempting to convince someone to give them an allowance, it would be important to state facts to support their opinions.

3. Explain to students that when writing to persuade, the writer tries to convince the reader(s) that his opinion is the best one. He states his opinion at the beginning; gives details or reasons that prove, explain, or support it; and concludes by restating his opinion.

4. Read aloud the prompt above, display it on a transparency, or write it on the board.

5. Give each student a copy of page 25. Have him use the reproducible to organize his thoughts and ideas.

Write It!

1. Instruct each student to use the information recorded on page 25 to write a paragraph persuading his parents to give him an allowance. Remind the student to include a topic sentence, at least three strong supporting details, and a concluding sentence.

2. Direct the student to proofread and edit his work carefully. Encourage students to swap papers to peer-edit. After all corrections have been made, have each student write his final copy on a half sheet of lined paper.

3. If desired, give each student a 4½" x 6" sheet of light green construction paper. Have him glue his final copy on the paper and then add details to make it resemble money. Display the money on a bulletin board decorated with construction paper fishhooks and titled "Angling for an Allowance."

Angling for an Allowance

Opinion/Topic Sentence:
_____
_____
_____

Supporting Details:

① _____

② _____

③ _____

④ _____

⑤ _____

Conclusion: _____

Highlights in History

The curator of the National History Museum is creating a display honoring the most important historical event of the 20th century. Choose an event; then write a paragraph persuading the curator to honor the event you've chosen.

Think It!

1. Guide students in brainstorming important historical events of the 20th century (for example, man landing on the moon and the Wright brothers' first successful flight). Then have students give reasons why these events are considered important.

2. From the reasons given, have students identify which are facts and which are opinions. Point out to students that when attempting to convince some-one of something, it is important to state facts to support your opinion.

3. Explain to students that when writing to persuade, the writer tries to convince the reader(s) that her opinion is the best one. She states her opinion at the beginning; gives details or reasons that prove, explain, or support it; and concludes by re-stating her opinion.

4. Read aloud the prompt above, display it on a transparency, or write it on the board. Have each student choose a 20th-century event that she thinks is the most important.

5. Give each student a copy of page 27. Instruct the student to use the reproducible to organize her thoughts and ideas.

Write It!

1. Have each student use the information recorded on page 27 to help write a persuasive paragraph to the museum curator on another sheet of paper. Remind the student to include a topic sentence, at least three strong supporting details, and a concluding sentence.

2. Direct the student to proofread and edit her work carefully. Encourage students to swap papers to peer-edit. After all corrections have been made, have the student write her final copy on another sheet of paper.

3. If desired, give each student a 12" x 18" sheet of yellow construction paper. Direct the student to cut the sheet in half. On one half of the sheet, have the student glue her final copy. On the other half, have the student cut out an oval that resembles a spotlight and then draw and color a picture of a museum display that highlights the historic event she selected. Display students' completed work on a bulletin board titled "Highlights in History."

Name

Highlights in History

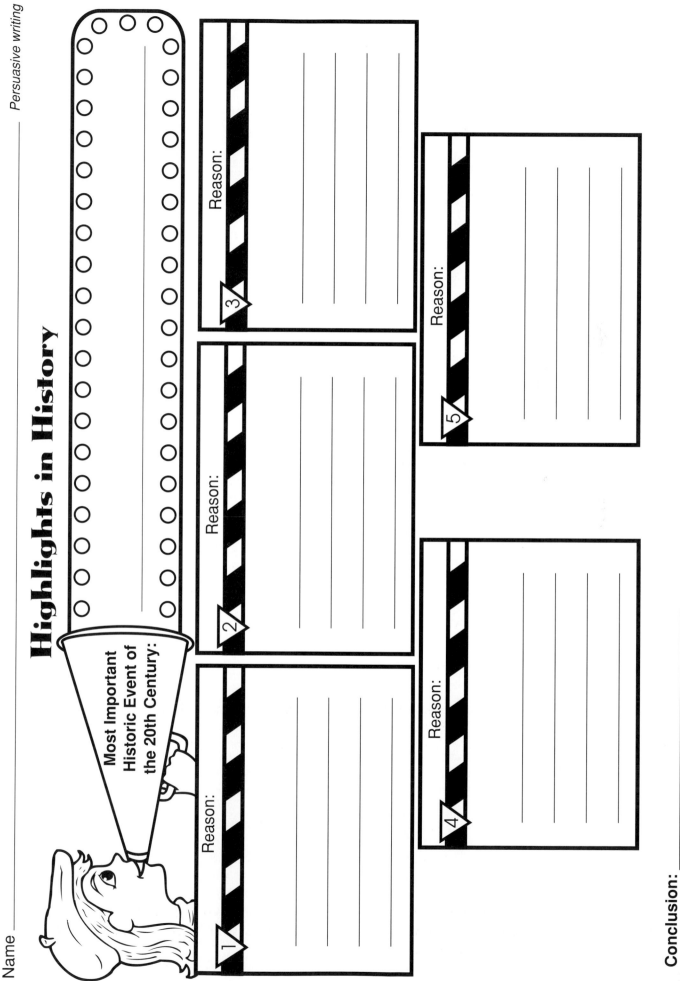

Most Important Historic Event of the 20th Century:

Reason: 1

Reason: 2

Reason: 3

Reason: 4

Reason: 5

Conclusion:

Road to Recycling

PROMPT *Reduce, reuse, recycle! Your community has started a recycling program, but many people aren't participating. Write a paragraph persuading people to recycle.*

Think It!

1. Pair students and have each pair list five classroom and five household objects that could be recycled.

2. As a class, brainstorm reasons why people should recycle. Record student responses on the board, having students identify each factual reason. Point out to students that when attempting to convince someone of something, it is important to state facts to support your opinion.

3. Explain to students that when writing to persuade, the writer tries to convince the reader(s) that his opinion is the best one. He states his opinion at the beginning; gives details or reasons that prove, explain, or support it; and concludes by restating his opinion.

4. Read aloud the prompt above, display it on a transparency, or write it on the board.

5. Give each student a copy of page 29. Have him use the reproducible to organize his thoughts and ideas about why people should recycle.

Write It!

1. Instruct each student to use the information recorded on page 29 to help write his paragraph. Remind the student to include a topic sentence, at least three strong supporting details, and a concluding sentence.

2. Direct the student to proofread and edit his work carefully. Encourage students to swap papers to peer-edit. After all corrections have been made, have each student write his final copy in the space provided on page 29.

3. If desired, have each student cut out the pattern along the bold lines and then color it and fold it along the thin lines to create a brochure. Lend the brochures to a younger class so they too can learn about the importance of recycling.

Name

Road to Recycling

Get on the Road to Recycling!

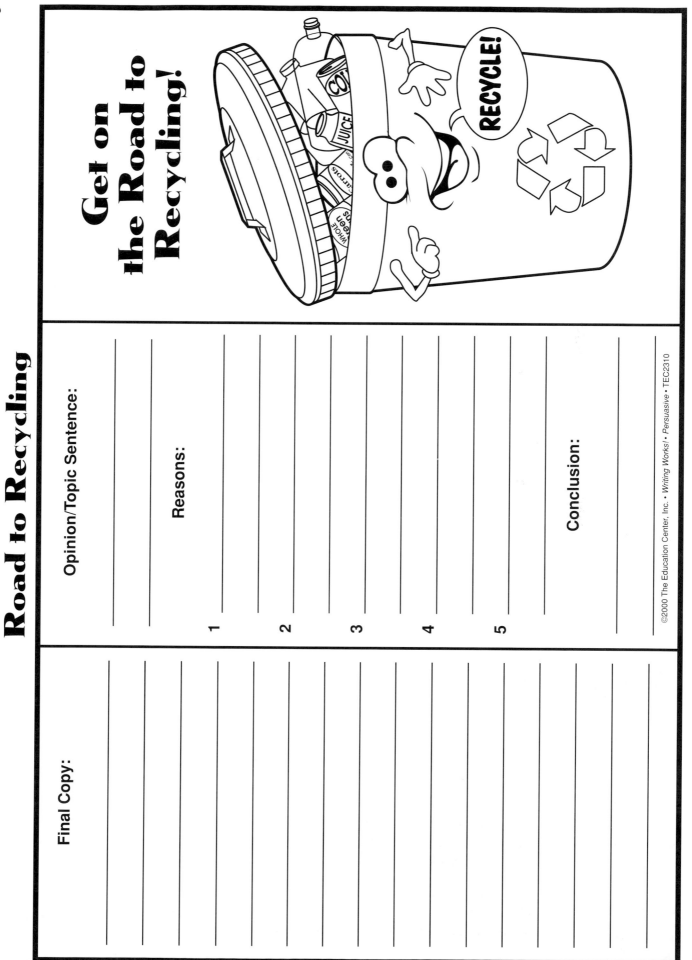

RECYCLE!

Opinion/Topic Sentence:

Reasons:

1

2

3

4

5

Conclusion:

Final Copy:

Camp Weneedsomoola

PROMPT Your friends are going to Camp Weneedsomoola for a week this summer. You have no money saved and the only way you can go is if your parents pay for it. Write a letter to your parents persuading them to pay for camp.

Think It!

1. Have students name some favorite activities, such as soccer, ballet, or in-line skating. Then tell students to imagine that in order to participate in one of these activities, they will have to borrow money from their parents.

2. Have students list reasons they would give their parents as to why they should receive the money. Record students' responses on the board. Point out to students that when attempting to persuade someone of something, it is important to state facts to support your opinion.

3. Explain to students that when writing to persuade, the writer tries to convince the reader(s) that her opinion is the best one. She states her opinion at the beginning; gives details or reasons that prove, explain, or support it; and concludes by restating her opinion.

4. Read aloud the prompt above, display it on a transparency, or write it on the board.

5. Give each student a copy of page 31. Have the student use the reproducible to organize her thoughts and ideas.

Write It!

1. On another sheet of paper, have the student use the information recorded on page 31 to help write a letter to her parents persuading them to give her money for camp. Remind the student to include a topic sentence, at least three strong supporting details, and a concluding sentence.

2. Direct the student to proofread and edit her work carefully. Encourage students to swap papers to peer-edit. After all corrections have been made, have the student write her final version on a separate sheet of paper.

3. If desired, provide each student with a construction paper T-shirt cutout. On one side of the cutout, have the student design a T-shirt for Camp Weneedsomoola. On the other side, have the student glue her letter. Then attach a length of string or yarn along a wall. After students share their letters, hang the T-shirts on the "clothesline" using clothespins.

Name _____   *Persuasive writing*

Camp Weneedsomoola

Opinion/Topic Sentence: _____

_____

Reasons You Should Send Me to Camp Weneedsomoola:

1

2

3

4

Conclusion: _____

_____

Field Trip Fever!

Imagine that you only get one field trip this year. The good news is that you get to decide where you go—and the sky's the limit! But there is one condition: you have to persuade your teacher that your field trip is an educational one!

Think It!

1. Have your students brainstorm a list of possible sites for a field trip. Record their responses on the board. Have student volunteers give reasons why they like the sites named.

2. Tell students your first choice for a field trip. Give reasons why it's your first choice, including some facts and some opinions. Point out to students that if you were attempting to convince someone that this was the best site, it would be important to state facts to support your opinion.

3. Explain to students that when writing to persuade someone, the writer tries to convince the reader(s) that his opinion is the best one. He states his opinion at the beginning; gives details or reasons that prove, explain, or support it; and concludes by restating his opinion.

4. Read aloud the prompt above, display it on a transparency, or write it on the board.

5. Give each student a copy of page 33. Have the student use the reproducible to organize his thoughts and ideas. Remind him that the reasons he gives for his choice must be educational ones.

Write It!

1. Instruct the student to use the information recorded on page 33 to help write a letter persuading his teacher that his field trip choice is the best one. Have him complete his letter on another sheet of paper. Remind the student to include a topic sentence, at least three strong supporting details, and a concluding sentence.

2. Direct the student to proofread and edit his work carefully. Encourage students to swap papers to peer-edit. After all corrections have been made, have the student write his final copy on another sheet of paper.

3. If desired, gather some items from potential field trip sites, such as brochures, ticket stubs from movies or other events, and playbills. Post these items, along with students' letters, onto a bulletin board. Title the display "Field Trip Fever!"

Persuasive writing

Field Trip Fever!

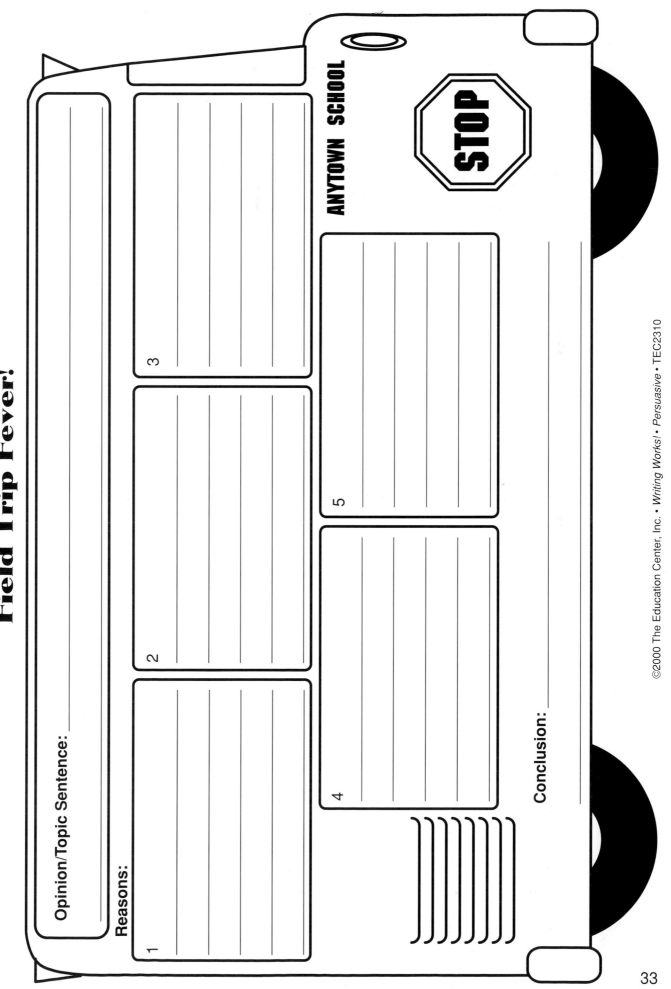

Opinion/Topic Sentence: _____

Reasons:

1.

2.

3.

4.

5.

ANYTOWN SCHOOL

STOP

Conclusion: _____

Dynamite Donations

PROMPT *Your class has raised some money to give to a charitable organization. Several possible organizations have been picked. Write a paragraph persuading your class that the charity you've chosen should get the money.*

Think It!

1. Have students brainstorm charitable groups and organizations (for example, food banks, homeless shelters, animal shelters). Record their responses on the board. Encourage students to give reasons why they would help these organizations if they were giving a donation.

2. Name an organization to which you give or would consider giving money. Give reasons why you'd give money to that organization, using facts and opinions. Point out to students that when attempting to convince someone of something, it is important to state facts to support your opinion.

3. Explain to students that when writing to persuade someone, the writer tries to convince the reader(s) that her opinion is the best one. She states her opinion at the beginning; gives details or reasons that prove, explain, or support it; and concludes by restating her opinion.

4. Read aloud the prompt above, display it on a transparency, or write it on the board.

5. Give each student one copy of page 35. Have the student use the reproducible to organize her thoughts and ideas.

Write It!

1. Instruct the student to use the information recorded on page 35 to help write a paragraph persuading her class that her choice for the charitable donation is the best one. Have her write her paragraph on a separate sheet of paper. Remind the student to include a topic sentence, at least three strong supporting details, and a concluding sentence.

2. Direct the student to proofread and edit her work carefully. Encourage students to swap papers to peer-edit. After all corrections have been made, have the student write her final copy on another sheet of paper.

3. If desired, fill a large jar with a supply of play money. Set up the jar along with students' paragraphs at a center titled "Dynamite Donations." Students will have fun guessing how much money has been "donated" and reading the different arguments about where this money should go.

Dynamite Donations

Opinion/Topic Sentence:

_____

_____

Supporting Details:

1

2

TNT

TNT

3

4

5

TNT

TNT

TNT

Conclusion: _____

_____

Trying Television

PROMPT *A study has shown that children spend too much time watching TV. To solve the problem, community leaders are asking parents to turn off the television. Write a paragraph persuading your parents to allow you to watch TV.*

Think It!

1. Ask students to estimate the number of hours they spent watching TV last week. Have them list reasons why they think this time was well spent.

2. Tell students that you think people should watch less television. Give reasons why, including some facts and some opinions. Point out to students that when attempting to convince someone of something, it is important to state facts to support your opinion.

3. Explain to students that when writing to persuade someone, the writer tries to convince the reader(s) that his opinion is the best one. He states his opinion at the beginning; gives details or reasons that prove, explain, or support it; and concludes by restating his opinion.

4. Read aloud the prompt above, display it on a transparency, or write it on the board.

5. Give each student a copy of page 37. Have the student use the reproducible to organize his thoughts and ideas.

Write It!

1. Instruct the student to use the information recorded on page 37 to help write a paragraph persuading his parents to allow him to watch TV. Have him write his paragraph on another sheet of paper. Remind the student to include a topic sentence, at least three strong supporting details, and a concluding sentence.

2. Direct the student to proofread and edit his work carefully. Encourage students to swap papers to peer-edit. After all corrections have been made, have the student write his final copy on another sheet of paper.

3. If desired, give each student a 12" x 18" sheet of light-colored construction paper. Instruct the student to glue his paragraph onto the center of the construction paper and then decorate the sheet to look like a TV set (with his paragraph representing the screen). Post the finished projects on a wall or bulletin board titled "Trying Television."

Name _____ *Persuasive writing*

Trying Television

Opinion/Topic Sentence:

Supporting Details:

1

2

3

4

5

Conclusion: _____

Fun With the Family? You Bet!

PROMPT *Your family is going on an outing! Having everyone in your family agree on an activity, however, might take some work. Write a paragraph persuading your family that your idea for family fun is the best one.*

Think It!

1. Have students name some of their favorite things to do with their families (go to a movie, to an amusement park, on a picnic, etc.). Record their responses on the board. Challenge them to give reasons why these activities are so much fun.

2. Tell students what your favorite family activity is. Give reasons why it is your favorite, using facts and opinions. Point out to students that when attempting to convince someone of something, it is important to state facts to support your opinion.

3. Explain to students that when writing to persuade someone, the writer tries to convince the reader(s) that her opinion is the best one. She states her opinion at the beginning; gives details or reasons that prove, explain, or support it; and concludes by restating her opinion.

4. Read aloud the prompt above, display it on a transparency, or write it on the board.

5. Give each student a copy of page 39. Have the student use the reproducible to organize her thoughts and ideas.

Write It!

1. Instruct the student to use the information recorded on page 39 to help write a paragraph persuading her family that her idea for the family outing is the best one. Have her write her paragraph on another sheet of paper. Remind the student to include a topic sentence, at least three strong supporting details, and a concluding sentence.

2. Direct the student to proofread and edit her work carefully. Encourage students to swap papers to peer-edit. After all corrections have been made, have the student write her final copy on a sheet of paper.

3. If desired, give each student a 9" x 12" sheet of white construction paper. Direct the student to draw, color, and cut out a road sign (a rectangle, an inverted triangle, an octagon, etc.). Encourage her to write a fitting phrase on her sign, such as "5 miles to amusement park" or "STOP here for the best restaurant!" Post each student's final copy on a wall or bulletin board, placing her sign atop her paragraph as a cover. Title the display "Fun With the Family? You Bet!"

Fun With the Family? You Bet!

Opinion/ Topic Sentence:

Supporting Details:

1

2

3

4

5

Conclusion:

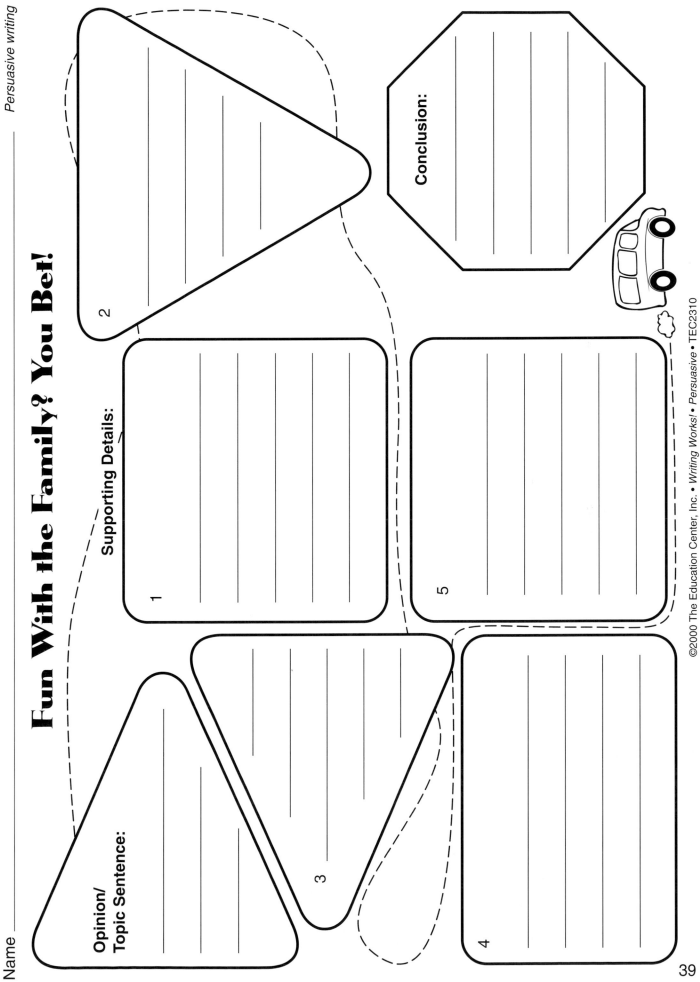

The Law of the Leash

PROMPT *Several dogs have been running loose around your neighborhood. Your community is hoping to get a leash law passed. Write a letter to community officials persuading them to pass the law.*

Think It!

1. Ask students to list several laws that are in effect in your area *(wearing bike safety helmets, no jaywalking, yielding to pedestrians in crosswalks)*. Discuss each law and the possible reasons why it may have been enacted.

2. Write the following sentences on the board:
   • It's good to have a law that requires bicyclists to wear helmets.
   • It's good to have a law that requires bicyclists to wear helmets because helmets protect the head from serious injury.
   Ask students, "If you were trying to convince someone that this law is reasonable which sentence do you think would be more effective?" Point out to students that sentence two is more effective because a fact is used to support the opinion.

3. Explain to students that when writing to persuade, the writer tries to convince the reader(s) that his opinion is the best one. He states his opinion at the beginning; gives details or reasons that prove, explain, or support it; and concludes by restating his opinion.

4. Read aloud the prompt above, display it on a transparency, or write it on the board.

5. Give each student a copy of page 41. Have the student use the reproducible to organize his thoughts and ideas.

Write It!

1. Direct the student to use the information recorded on page 41 to help write a letter persuading community officials that a leash law should be passed. Remind the student to include a topic sentence, at least three strong supporting details, and a concluding sentence.

2. Direct the student to proofread and edit his work carefully. Encourage students to swap papers to peer-edit. After all corrections have been made, have the student write his final copy of the letter on another sheet of paper.

3. If desired, make an enlarged copy of the dog character on page 41. Have student volunteers create four leashes from construction paper. Attach the character and the leashes to a bulletin board as shown on the reproducible. Post students' letters in clusters at the ends of the leashes.

Name

The Law of the Leash

Opinion/Topic Sentence:

Reason 1:

Reason 2:

Reason 3:

Reason 4:

Conclusion:

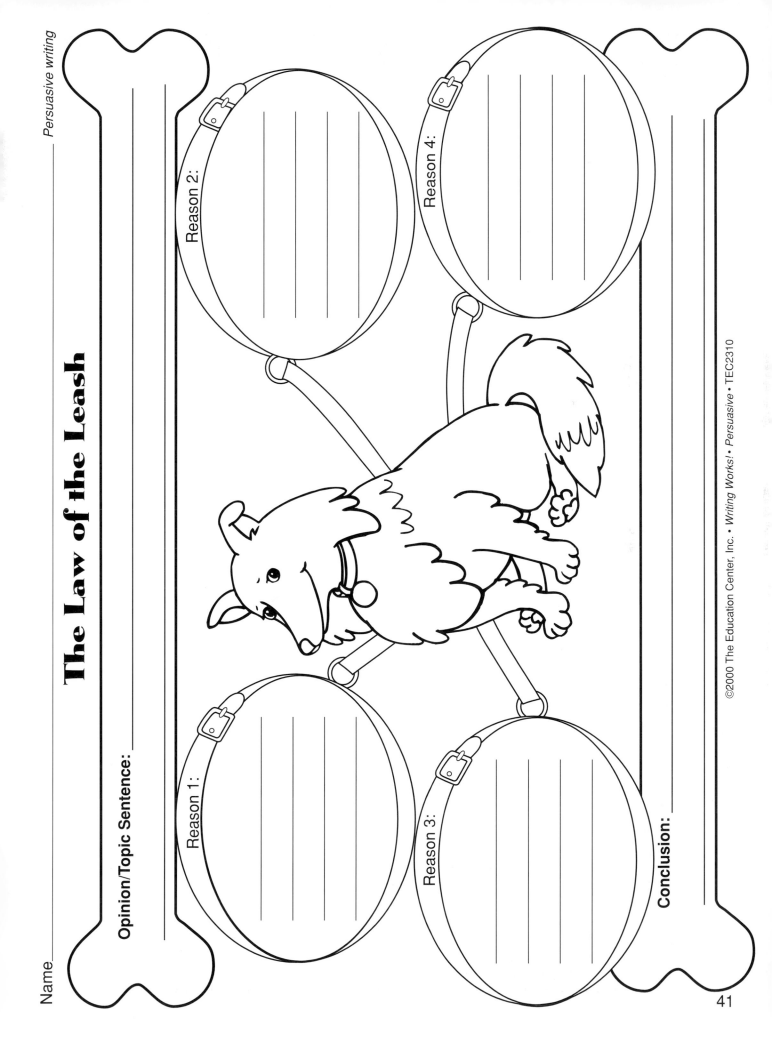

Go, Mascot!

PROMPT
Your school is selecting a new mascot. The selection committee wants to choose a mascot that will best represent your school. Write a letter persuading the committee that your mascot choice is the best one.

Think It!

1. Have students name the mascots of their favorite sports teams. Record their responses on the board. Challenge them to explain why each organization may have chosen its particular mascot.

2. Tell students what your favorite team is and what its mascot is. Give reasons why the mascot is an appropriate choice, using facts and opinions. Point out to students that when attempting to convince someone of something, it is important to state facts to support your opinion.

3. Explain to students that when writing to persuade someone, the writer tries to convince the reader(s) that her opinion is the best one. She states her opinion at the beginning; gives details or reasons that prove, explain, or support it; and concludes by restating her opinion.

4. Read aloud the prompt above, display it on a transparency, or write it on the board.

5. Give each student a copy of page 43. Have the student use the reproducible to organize her thoughts and ideas.

Write It!

1. Instruct the student to use the information recorded on page 43 to help write a letter persuading the selection committee that her choice for the school mascot is the best one. Have her write her letter on another sheet of paper. Remind the student to include a topic sentence, at least three strong supporting details, and a concluding sentence.

2. Direct the student to proofread and edit her work carefully. Encourage students to swap papers to peer-edit. After all corrections have been made, have the student write her final copy on a sheet of paper.

3. If desired, give each student a pennant cut out of light-colored construction paper. Have the student draw and color a picture of the new mascot on the pennant. Then display the pennants, along with the completed letters, where others can enjoy them.

Go, Mascot!

**Opinion/
Topic Sentence:** _____
_____

**Supporting
Details:**

1. _____
_____
_____

2. _____
_____
_____

3. _____
_____

4. _____
_____
_____

5. _____
_____

Conclusion: _____
_____

Proofreading Checklist

To the Student: Use this checklist during the proofreading or editing stage of your writing to help you determine what needs improving and/or correcting before writing the final version. Then give this checklist and your writing to a peer editor (a classmate) to use to edit your work.

Title of Writing Selection:_____

Things to Check	Writer's Checklist		Peer Editor's Checklist	
	Yes	No	Yes	No
1. Does the writing have a topic sentence and a concluding sentence?				
2. Does the writing clearly state the opinion?				
3. Do the details or reasons prove, explain, or support the opinion?				
4. Are factual details or reasons used?				
5. Does the writing make sense and is it easy to read?				
6. Did the writer use strong nouns, adjectives, and verbs?				
7. Does each sentence begin with a capital letter?				
8. Does each sentence have an ending punctuation mark?				
9. Did the writer use complete sentences?				
10. Did the writer check for misspelled words?				
11. Is each paragraph indented?				

☆ If the peer editor checked "No" in any box above, discuss it with the editor.

Think About It!

I think I did a _____ job on this writing selection because…

_____

_____

Persuasive-Writing Assessment

Student's Name: _____ **Date:** _____

Title of Writing: _____

Assessment Items	Agree	Disagree
1. The writing selection has a topic sentence and concluding sentence.		
2. The writing selection persuades someone of something.		
3. The topic sentence clearly states an opinion.		
4. The details or reasons prove, explain, or support the opinion.		
5. Factual details are used.		
6. All details relate to the topic.		
7. The writing selection makes sense; it is easy to read.		
8. Strong nouns, adjectives, and verbs are used.		
9. Correct punctuation and capitalization are used.		
10. Each word is spelled correctly.		
11. Run-on sentences and incomplete sentences are avoided.		
12. Each verb agrees with its subject.		
13. All proper nouns are capitalized.		
14. Each paragraph is indented.		
15. Apostrophes are correctly used to form contractions and to show possession.		

Comments: _____

_____

_____

_____

_____

Extra Prompts

1. Your parents are buying a brand-new automobile! They want your opinion about which one to buy—a luxury car, a minivan, or a sport-utility vehicle. Write a paragraph to your parents persuading them to buy one of the vehicles.

2. Your friends are all getting their own personal telephones, but your parents think it is a waste of money. Write a letter to your parents persuading them to let you get a phone of your own.

3. Your grade-level classmates are hosting a school dance. They can't decide which musical group to invite to perform. Write a paragraph persuading your classmates to choose your favorite group.

4. The local humane society is trying to get citizens to adopt some of its animals. Write a persuasive paragraph promoting the adoption of these pets. Give reasons that explain the advantages of owning a pet from the pound.

5. You and your friends want to get together this weekend. The only problem is, you can't agree on what to do. Choose an activity; then write a letter to your friends convincing them to agree with you.

6. Summer is here and you want to get a job to earn a little extra spending money. But your parents aren't quite sure they want to allow you to do this. Write a paragraph to your parents persuading them to let you get a summertime job.

7. The mayor of your city is trying to decide if a 7:00 P.M. curfew for children under the age of 14 is needed. What do you think? Write a letter to the mayor to convince him or her to enact, or not to enact, the curfew.

8. Your normal bedtime is 9:30 P.M. There is a 10:00 movie that you want to see tonight. Write a paragraph persuading your parents to let you stay up and watch the movie.

Extra Prompts

9. You and a friend are trying to decide what birthday present to get another friend. Choose a gift that you think is the best one. Then write a letter to your friend persuading him or her to agree with your choice.

10. Your class has been asked to create a school display honoring the most important president in American history. There is disagreement as to which president that is. Write a paragraph to your classmates persuading them to agree with your choice.

11. Your family is getting ready to move to a new home and your parents have given you two choices: in a neighborhood outside a city or on a farm in the country. Where would you like to live? Write a paragraph to your family persuading them to live either outside the city or on a farm.

12. In order to save money, your principal is thinking about canceling all field trips for the remainder of the year! Write a letter to your principal persuading him or her to allow students to continue taking field trips.

13. A close member of your family recently won one million dollars in the lottery. What do you think this person should do with the money? Write a paragraph persuading your relative to agree with you.

14. Recent bad weather has caused school cancellations. Your principal has given students a choice between longer school days or Saturday school in order to make up the days. Write a paragraph to your classmates persuading them to agree with your choice.

15. Imagine that your mother is planning a holiday meal. She will prepare either a turkey or a ham for the main course. Write a paragraph persuading your mother to prepare your favorite meat.

16. Your friends are planning a super skiing weekend, but your parents are not sure whether they should let you go. Write a paragraph to your parents convincing them to let you go.

Editing Symbols

Writers use special marks called *editing symbols* to help them edit and revise their work. Editing symbols are used to show what changes a writer wants to make in his or her writing.

Symbol	Meaning	Example
⬭	Correct spelling.	⬭animl
ℓ	Delete or remove.	dogg ℓ
◡	Close the gap.	fi◡sh
∧	Add a letter or word.	lives in tree a ∧ ∧
#	Make a space.	flies#south
⌐⌐	Reverse the order of a letter, a word, or words.	plants eats
∧	Insert a comma.	the crab an arthropod ∧ ∧
⊙	Insert a period.	Cats purr⊙
∨	Insert an apostrophe.	a deer∨s antlers
∨∨ ∨∨	Insert quotation marks.	She said, ∨∨Look at the pig.∨∨
≡	Make the letter a capital.	≡birds eat seeds.
/	Make the letter lowercase.	a /Snowshoe hare
¶	Start a new paragraph.	¶Some dogs have tails.